Beauty of
Missouri

Beauty of
Missouri

Text: Paul M. Lewis
Concept & Design: Robert D. Shangle

First Printing October, 1990
Published by LTA Publishing Company
2735 S.E. Raymond Street, Portland, Oregon 97202
Robert D. Shangle, Publisher

"Learn about America in a beautiful way."

Library of Congress Cataloging-in-Publication Data

Lewis, Paul M.

The Beauty of Missouri / text, Paul M. Lewis

    p.   cm.

  ISBN 1-55988-005-8: $19.95. — ISBN 1-55988-004-X (pbk.): $9.95

   1. Missouri — Description and travel — 1981 — Views.

2. Missouri — Description and travel — 1981 — Guide-books.

I. Title.

F467.L49   1989

917.7804'43 — dc20   89-38294

CIP

Contents

The Missouri Waltz

It's hard to settle on any one label to size up neatly the state of Missouri. Even Missouri's role in the affairs of the nation has changed over the years. For a long time it was the western edge of the country, wild and unknown Indian territory across one colossal river and drained by another. After the exploits of Lewis and Clark galvanized the infant nation into a great move westward, eastern Missouri changed from a lonely outpost to an advance way station and outfitter for the stream of pioneers bound for the Louisiana Purchase lands and beyond.

Missouri became a state in 1821. In the 1840s its western communities took over the role of staging area, this time for the great caravans of wagon trains bound for the Far West, the land beyond the Rockies. In mid-century, when the California Gold Rush threatened to tilt the continent into the Pacific Ocean, Missouri's central position and St. Louis' commercial know-how in equipping and guiding the parties of would-be miners helped the state to a new spurt of growth.

The years preceding the Civil War were unsettled and tumultuous for Missouri. Slavery was permitted in the state, and a strong pro-South sentiment had developed among the slave-holders, who were a minority, but politically powerful. The slavery advocates were concentrated along the Missouri River and in the southeast. But other Missourians were pushing for abolition, most of these living and working in the St. Louis commercial sphere. These Missourians were now in the majority, working-class citizens who had been born in the Old Country. Their objections to slavery were mainly economic, based on the competition of slave labor. Most Missourians were for a compromise of the slavery issue, but when the war at last erupted, the state was split into pro-Union and pro-South factions. Missouri was secured for the Union early in the war, but Southern sympathizers and guerillas were constantly active in the southeast, south, and west.

The movements of war supplies had done a lot for Missouri's growth, as had the various migratory drives. Now, in spite of being on the country's two biggest rivers, the state was no longer dependent on them for its commerce. St. Louis had become a great railroad terminus, and rootin'-tootin' Kansas City was getting fat supplying the needs of settlers in some of the new western states. Missouri rapidly developed two opposing personalities. As the century neared its close, business and industry became more and more concentrated in a few urban centers, notably Kansas City and St. Louis. With a strong agricultural base already long established, the rural-urban opposites began to pull against each other in a "war" that still goes on in the state councils of government and in other phases of Missouri life.

Another oddity. Missouri is a serene, quiet, restful, beautiful place. But it's ambitious and restless, too, eager to turn its mineral resources and natural charms to practical use. The individual Missourian is deeply involved in the equation. He is a very hospitable person, usually unfailingly courteous to strangers in his midst. But one wouldn't be wise to mistake his friendly curiosity for unconcern about his own welfare. The state was, after all, settled by a wild mixture of national types who had to co-exist successfully. So shrewdness, competitiveness, and independent thinking are practically built into the Missourian who traces his in-state lineage back at least a few generations. The Missouri mule is famous everywhere as the epitome of mulish superiority in strength and disposition to the ordinary run of mules. It is good to think there might be a touch of amiable calculation in his character, too, to match up with an ingredient in the makeup of the Missourian who raised him.

Many people speak of an unexplainable *something* that seems to prowl the Missouri landscape, be it river scene, Ozark hill, deep woods, rolling prairie, or quiet little town. The author MacKinlay Kantor, a long-time Missouri-lover, talks about an incompleteness, a spooky feeling that something else is waiting in the wings. The *unexpected* seems to be the only routine thing in Missouri. Who would have thought that an eastern Missouri river town would have produced one of the immortals of American literature? Yet, as Mark Twain might have said, immodestly, "Why not?" And who would have thought that western Missouri would have nurtured a man who some believe will be ranked with the greatest leaders in American history? There you *really* have the unexpected, since Harry Truman was Harry *Who?* when he took over the country after the death of a president who was revered almost as a god.

So Missouri is so much more than a state that just happens to be located in the core of the country's heartland. It is the dynamic center of a dynamic nation. The Missouri story is a story of widely different elements blending into a society that pulses with the drive to get ahead, to do the things that need to be done. Isn't that the idea that moves the whole country, that has goaded it through the years into accomplishments beyond those of any previous civilization? Missouri is the pattern for the other 49. Even the states that are senior to it look with admiration on its example. For Missouri is the bellwether by which the rest of the nation sets its course.

P.M.L.

The Missouri Ozarks

The Ozark highlands of Missouri begin south of the Missouri River and go all the way to the border. After that they're the Arkansas Ozarks. The Missouri portion reaches its highest point in the St. François highlands of the eastern Ozarks, an irregular jumble of knobby masses topped off by Taum Sauk Mountain at 1,772 feet. West to east, they begin at the prairie land around Joplin and range over to the Mississippi River bottom lands in the southeastern corner. The eastern region is big spring country, and here, too, are some of the strangest shapes, such as those in Elephant Rocks State Park at Graniteville, where once sharp-angled formations have been worn away to bulbous, potato shapes of tremendous size.

The Ozark hills, ancient remnants of once tall mountains, have been laid low over a period of years so long that the number reads something like the national debt. In that big hunk of time, the mountains have not only shrunk into hills, but have acquired some weird and wonderful characteristics. In east-central and southeast Missouri, especially, they are riddled with caves, faced with bluffs, afloat in subterranean streams, and awash with some of the biggest springs in the country. The very biggest of the springs is named, with remarkable clarity, "Big Spring." Its flow is believed to be the largest in the United States for a single source — more than 840-million gallons daily.

The Ozark's springs are as varied in color as they are in size. Their waters are crystal clear, pale blue, turquoise, or jade green. In the same region as Big Spring are Round and Alley springs, all in the heart of the eastern Ozark backwoods. Farther north are Meramec Springs, one of the three famous landmarks in the area that includes a cave and a river. The springs are a hundred or so miles southwest of St. Louis in a little wooded valley. They give their waters up to the Meramec River nearby. The river flows up from the south-central Ozarks in a northeasterly direction, curving around the southern perimeter of St. Louis and emptying into the Mississippi. St. Louisans appreciate the proximity of the stream, and make varied recreational use of it, including fishing (the Indian name, *Meramec*, means "catfish"). Before it got so sportive, the Meramec was all business. It was a highway into the country west of the Mississippi River for French and American settlers, as well as a transportation route for trade. Lead deposits were discovered in the 1700s along the banks of the lower river, attracting settlement into the region.

The Meramec Cavern, or Caverns, open into a big bluff that rises from the river gorge fifty-some miles southwest of St. Louis, outside of the town of Stanton. The various caves have become a favorite target for visitors since they were opened to the public in 1936. Before that they were handy hiding places for some of the less orthodox Missouri citizenry, among them Jesse James. These caverns depart from the normal habit of such openings to burrow down into the earth. They reach up high into the bluff to 240 feet, divided among several floors.

Here in the eastern Ozarks are some scenic rivers, the first of the nation to be so designated by law. The Ozark National Scenic Riverways covers, with its protective umbrella, long stretches of the big Current River, its tributary, Jacks Fork, and other streams in the system, in all of their original natural beauty. The wilderness isolation of these waters and woods makes possible the fullest enjoyment of a popular Missouri pastime: float trips. The Current River, with its authoritative flow, is highly regarded for these kinds of enchantments. The river's specialties are fishing and scenery-watching, and the guided float trips are well-suited for these. The Current, in the vicinity of Round and Big Springs, is where the best of the float-fishing is done. Trips sometimes last for several days, and fishing parties camp at night on sand bars where the river bends. The sparsely settled neighborhood around Big Springs has tourist accommodations for prospective floaters. Visitors are warmly welcomed.

The Current River follows a long, twisting, sometimes lively course through the Ozark backwoods, eventually hitching up with the Black River a few miles over the border into Arkansas. The Black River is a Missouri stream, too, along the upper river. The Black rises to the east of the Current, over some narrow, sharply defined, and deep valleys. Still farther eastward is the St. Francis River, another of the eastern Ozarks' big streams. These three major waterways have cut deep gaps in the dividing ridges of this complex country of hills and rolling plateaus. Two big flood control reservoirs, Clearwater on the Black River and Wappapello on the St. Francis, provide their own share of fishing and boating opportunities.

The Osage River flows more than halfway across Missouri from west to east like the big Missouri River, up to a point. The point being just east of Jefferson City, where the Osage joins the bigger river instead of just following along a varying number of miles to the south. The Osage is no mere trickle either, but big and athletic like the Indians of the tribe it is named for.

At the northern limits of the Ozark hills, the Osage has been impounded since 1931, by Bagnell Dam, forming a lake that has become one of the recreational meccas for Missouri. Looking like a dragon with a thousand legs, Lake of the Ozarks curves and twists for 129 miles into the valleys carved by the streams that drain into the Osage. As a consequence, the lake's shoreline is measured at 1,300 miles.

Most of the long and intricate shoreline is rimmed by undisturbed forest land. The drowned valleys were cleared of trees when the dam was built, so the dense surrounding woods descend just to the water line. The effect is of nature and man collaborating, this time with happy results.

You can go fishing on the Big Dragon, or just go visiting on it, and take weeks to cover all of its coves and beaches. The thrill is not only in floating over its sometimes-blue waters. Part of the excitement of the lake can be associated with some of the towns on its banks. There are a few very commercially-oriented towns around the lake's perimeter, such as Lake Ozark and Camdenton on the eastern end, and Warsaw in the west at the head of the lake. Warsaw was a river town before it became a lakeside community. In its former life it was not quite as upright as it is these days when the town's livelihood is so dependent on the goodwill of the people who begin their Lake of the Ozarks vacations here. Warsaw has a history that might be too much excitement for vacationers, were it to be reenacted today.

When Warsaw was merely a riverside village on the Osage in the early 1800s, it had an important role in the commercial well-being of the Ozark region. Its position near the head of navigation gave Warsaw prominence as a shipping point. But that wasn't all that gave the town dramatic emphasis. About the middle of the century, Warsaw became the center of a region notable for its lawless types. The townspeople, literally, had to defend their society against an army of rustlers, horse thieves, and other criminals who had over the years increased their hold on the Ozark backwoods of Missouri. Up until the Civil War, the law was usually in the hands of those with the most guns. Finally, toward the end of the century, Warsaw lost its attraction for the lawless elements because river traffic had dropped off. It resumed its quiet village role, staying that way until the building of the Bagnell Dam gave it another life as a lakeside tourist resort.

Camdenton is on a southeastern arm of the lake, a community-come-lately as far as the towns in these parts are concerned. It was spawned in 1929 when the nearby town of Linn Creek had to move out of the way of the new lake's rising waters. The original townsite abandoned, Linn Creek couldn't quite decide where to settle. So, like an amoeba, it split in two, half of its inhabitants moving farther up the Niangua River valley and the other half choosing a commanding position on a nearby bluff for the new town of Camdenton. The newer settlement has now become the larger, and, in the bargain, the seat of Camden County, a county that has turned from cutting down its hickory, oak, and cedar trees for boards.

The county now prefers them on the vertical, the better to provide scenery and sanctuary. The scenery is furnished in truly spectacular fashion by the magnificent hardwood forests that reach in solid ranks back from the lake shores. And so is the sanctuary, in whose protective embrace lives an abundance of wildlife that has been drawn to this watery Ozark wonder and its environs.

Some miles south of the southernmost arm of the big lake is the town of Lebanon, one of the places on Interstate Highway 44 between Rolla and Springfield. When you get to Lebanon, you're pretty well immersed in Ozark country. The landscape is exceptionally beautiful and up until recent times was rather insulated from the bothersome outside world. But in spite of its relative isolation, Lebanon has not had a very quiet time of it. Before white settlers moved in from Tennessee, in the early 1800s, the place was home to the Osage Indians. The peaceful Osage were driven from their beautiful valley home by the Tennesseans. The new settlers quickly put their stamp on the place, making prosperous occupations out of preaching and moonshining. The latter profession has been considerably slowed by the Revenuers, but preaching is still widespread in Lebanon, as it is in most of the Ozark country. Lebanon has some forty churches to serve a population of about 10,000.

During the Civil War, Lebanon and some other Ozark settlements were fought over and captured by one or the other of the contending sides. Lebanon's position astride the important St. Louis-Springfield military road assured that things would be stirred up as long as the armies were pushing each other around in the area.

Springfield is deep into the Ozark hills, 55 miles to the southwest on the Interstate. It's the big city of the Ozarks and third largest of the whole state. Calling itself the "Gateway to the Southern Ozarks," Springfield is an entry to much of the "deep Ozark" magic and mystery. To the north is Pomme de Terre Lake, a junior-sized "dragon" created by a dam, but it manages to look as beautiful as lakes where nature did all the preparatory work. Northwest of Springfield is big Stockton lake, another many-armed

14

reservoir. South of the city, huge and intricate Table Rock Lake pokes its arms into the narrow valleys of the White River and its tributaries for 50 east-west miles. There is no telling how far Table Rock, looking on the map something like a compressed accordion, would stretch if it were straightened out.

The big White River folds into several other big-dragon lakes in this part of southern Missouri and northern Arkansas. The town of Branson, on Lake Taneycomo, the next reservoir east of Table Rock, has become the center of a thriving tourist area. The northern arms of Bull Shoals and Norfolk reservoirs, farther east, reach across the border from Arkansas. US Route 160 drops in to take a look at Taneycomo and the latter two, State Route 76 wanders around the vicinity of Table Rock, coming in from the southwest corner. People come from all over the country to taste the special qualities of these blue lakes, deep in the highland woods of southwestern Missouri. This area is equipped with handsome state parks, like Roaring River and Table Rock parks, which are wonderfully attuned to their unique surroundings.

Southern Ozark locales are loaded with Civil War memories. The destructive backwash of that prolonged struggle seeped into the richly wooded hills and hollows of this primitive countryside. It affected the big towns, too. Places like Joplin and Springfield were, in a way, hostage to the armies of both North and South that maneuvered and marched at various times in Ozark country. In those days Joplin was a mining camp on the western edge of the Ozark bulge, and extraction of lead and zinc — especially lead — was beginning to foreshadow greatness for Joplin as a town. But the military people had an immediate use for lead, and whatever was produced was appropriated for bullets. After the war, with the arrival of the railroads, mining made a prosperous town out of Joplin. After the nearby mines were exhausted, Joplin continued its growth. In this century it has become a regional economic center because of its strategic location at the edge of the great western plains and the Ozarks.

The Ozarks during the Civil War were almost denuded of backwoods settlers. Everybody gathered in the towns for protection, fleeing not the armies but the bushwhackers and other free-lance terrorists who pillaged, plundered, and worse in the vacuum left when the armies moved on. Only two major engagements were fought in the Missouri Ozarks — at Wilson's Creek, near Springfield, and at Pilot Knob in southeast Missouri. Springfield was in contention because of its key location and commercial prosperity. Wilson's Creek, 11 miles south, was the scene of a battle on August 10, 1861. The Confederate forces, at great cost, won the day, and consequently Springfield. They were evicted seven months later by Union troops. When the Feds returned, they brought with them Charles Butler, "Wild Bill" Hickok, who did some scouting and spying for the Union, and who later became a gun totin' United States marshal.

US Route 71, the main road south from Joplin, meanders through countryside that is downright "purty" in both its natural and manmade aspects. Neosho, just 17 miles along, Anderson, 28, and Noel, close to the Arkansas border on a side road, are towns whose beauty was planned and whose citizens take pride in their communities. Neosho is the big city of the thinly populated southwest corner, with about 9,800 on the rolls. It has a gracious, spacious charm given it by wide streets, venerable big trees, and extravagant displays of flowers during most of the year. Neosho became a lead mining town about 1850, like Joplin, when some productive mines were opened. The secessionist members of Missouri's legislature met in Neosho in October, 1861, and declared for the Confederacy. Their deliberations were interrupted by Federal troops and they adjourned to the town of Cassville, 50 miles southeast. Neosho, like other south Ozark communities, changed hands a couple of times during the war and didn't really find stability until after hostilities had ceased.

This edge-of-the-Ozarks country lacks the higher hills that are more typical of the interior but is no less endowed with entrancing natural features. Clear, pure streams wander through the wooded highlands, curving by big limestone bluffs. There are caves here, too, and small lakes, some inside the caves. In the dry caverns, visitors may sometimes indulge in "cave-crawling," a strenuous activity engaged in by people

16

Alley Springs Grist Mill, near Eminence

Lake Taneycomo, near Branson

Rose Garden, Missouri Botanical Garden, St. Louis

St. Louis

Bull Shoals Lake

Tower Grove Park, St. Louis

Farm near Dillard

Kansas City from Penn Valley Park

Mississippi River at Burlington

Hodgson Grist Mill, in the "Ozarks"

Lake Taneycomo

Bollinger Mill near Jackson

State Capitol Building, Jefferson City

In the "Ozarks," near Tecumseh

Mark Twain boyhood home, Hannibal

Central Missouri State University, Warrensburg

Table Rock Lake

Lake of the Ozarks

Historic St. Charles depot at St. Charles

Dawt Grist Mill, near Tecumseh

University of Missouri, Columbia

Lake of the Ozarks

Autumn in the Ozarks

Farm near Defiance

Lake of the Ozarks

Dillard Grist Mill

Harry S. Trman Library, Independence

Missouri River, west of Defiance

St. Louis skyline at day's end

St. Peter Church, Jefferson City

Historic First State Capitol Building, St. Charles

Near Eminence

The Climatron, Missouri Botanical Garden, St. Louis

Spirit of St. Charles river boat, St. Charles

Japanese Garden, Missouri Botanical Garden, St. Louis

Bollinger Covered Bridge near Jackson

Mississippi River near Hannibal

North Fork of the White River

"Old" Courthouse, St. Louis

Table Rock Lake and Kimberling City

"The Jewel Box," Forest Park, St. Louis

Lighthouse on Cardiff Hill, Hannibal

Forest Park, St. Louis

Zanoni Grist Mill near Gainesville

The Nelson-Atkins Art Museum, Kansas City

Sandy Creek Covered Bridge, south of St. Louis

Lake Buteo, Knob Noster State Park

Daniel Boone Home near Defiance

given to investigations of such places. This may be done in the vicinity of Lanagan and Pineville. Noel, in the same general neighborhood, specializes in a more sedate recreation, but just as adventurous. The little town sits by the Elk River and makes a part of its living from float trips conducted on that stream. As we have seen, float trips are popular on many Ozark waterways. Riding a canoe or john-boat, floaters glide along wooded banks from fishing hole to fishing hole, finding the good places with the help of local guides. With no help at all, they also enjoy the lush streamside scenery.

Not just the visitor, but the Ozark dweller goes for the quiet pleasure of riding a crystal-clear steam and breathing the sweet air that wraps the forest-and-river summer in a blanket of soft allurement. There are plenty of ol' swimmin' holes all over. Just take your choice. Those who know about these matters go swimming here with shoes on, and whatever else they may be wearing. Old canvas shoes are required gear to negotiate the gravelly beaches without pain. The spirit of Huck Finn certainly must preside over these Ozark sanctuaries. This is really Mark Twain country, with surprises and delights for anybody with a sense of history and a taste for adventure.

Along The Wide Missouri

If you didn't already know it, a quick look at a map of the United States will tell you that the Missouri River is not just a Missouri river. It flows through Montana, North Dakota, and South Dakota, between Iowa and Nebraska, then south along the three corners of Nebraska, Kansas, and Missouri before it swings east through its namesake state for the final part of that 2,700 mile career.

Kansas City is now the entryway for the river into Missouri. But of course the river took the same route for who knows how long before Kansas City was even a smudge on a map. In the east St. Louis has grown up just south of where the Missouri gives its water to the Mississippi. The city was a brawling frontier trading center in 1804, the year Lewis and Clark began their epochal exploration into the western territories, charting the course of the Missouri and Columbia rivers. The first part of their voyage, across what is now Missouri, was the most difficult. The big river, then as now, was shifty and treacherous, a turbid, mud-colored, surging stream of immense power and destructive potential. Its narrow channels were hemmed in by a maze of shallows, hidden rocks, and sand bars, and the current continally cut away at unstable banks. The Missouri is a little better behaved now because of dams and other flood control installations, but its power and perversity is no less for its domain having divided into states instead of being just unexplored wilderness.

The river did alright before there was a Kansas City, as we said. But it can't hurt to make a grand entrance, and K.C. provides it. One of the most vibrant and forward-looking of the nation's urban centers, Kans'

City (Missourians tend to drop a syllable) sort of erupted on the edge of the Great Plains in the middle of the 19th century. Its strategic position, on the big bend of the Missouri at a crossroads of the east-west commerce, established it from the start as a city with a future. Kansas City calls itself the "Heart of America", and with good reason. It has always had a reputation as a brash upstart, like the United States, waxing wealthy and a little wild on its trade in oil, wheat, and cattle. Once in a while, in the past, the cow-town image was hung on Kansas City. It has always been too busy with a number of things to have that rather demeaning phrase describe it with any accuracy. The town's prosperous, open, wheeler-dealer style of life has yielded to the sophistication of confident maturity. If Kansas City may have had a shady past, one would never know it now. The community is one of the country's cleanest, in every sense. Though still a hard-driving place, the big town is a beautiful one. It has some of the most impressive residential districts of any city in the country, along with its factories and furnaces, steel plants and stockyards. The beginnings are still visible in the old, but spruced-up, buildings of Westport Square, a reminder of the old town of Westport that in 1899 became a part of the new Kansas City.

This big crossroads town moderates its powerful push ahead by attention to origins, even though they are still part of a relatively recent past. Proud, but now grown a bit meditative, the city may be blending more of Missouri's "Show Me" motto with its dynamic move into the future. Its successful drive for supremacy in the heartland, and its moments of agony in a war that tore asunder Missouri and the nation, have given it a confidence mixed with caution. "Show me," says Kansas City, blending the old with the new in a prudent, if not skeptical, approach to the issues of today and tomorrow.

Before the Missouri River gets to Kansas City, it touches St. Joseph — "St. Joe", by common consent — a short hop to the north on the freeway. St. Joe is a good-sized place, about fourth among Missouri cities. But St. Joe was important before, and even, by a few years, before Kansas City was born. The town was established as a trading post early in the

19th century. Its position on the river as a communications link to the East helped bring it prosperity during the great migrations of settlers into the Oregon Territory at the century's mid-point. The completion of a cross-state railroad from St. Louis in 1859 insured St. Joseph's economic future. The Civil War brought a pause in the town's prosperity, but things picked up again after that war ended. With the arrival of peace, St. Joe became a livestock market of premier importance and the terminus of five more railroads. Like many Missouri River towns, it sits high up on bluffs, the better to foil that unpredictable stream when it gets mean and swollen with flood waters.

St. Joe is another place where the past is regarded with affection. Even Jesse James is remembered. His house, where he lived as "**Mr. Howard**", still stands here. So do some of the more important relics, including the house of Joseph Robidoux, the colorful founder of St. Joe. Born of French-Canadian parents, he left his native St. Louis around the turn of the century, established fur-trading posts along the upper Missouri, including St. Joseph. The settlement was called "Robidoux's Post" until the founder had a town platted in 1843 and gave it the name St. Joseph, his patron saint.

Other mementos of St. Joe's earlier days are the Pony Express Stables and the Indian artifacts collection in the St. Joseph Museum. St. Joe was, after all, an outpost for a long time in Indian lands, a frontier town where the Indians and pioneers lived in alternate states of peace and war. The Indians of the northwestern area challenged the settlers until 1836, when their lands were purchased and ceded to the new state of Missouri. The town is all the richer for keeping alive a part of the vanished Indian culture that was once so alive in the Midwest and Plains.

The muddy Missouri passes some interesting places on its turbulent journey across the state. Lexington comes up not far from Kansas City. It, too, predates the state of Missouri. Lexington was a ferry crossing before it was anything else. From a high perch where the river valley straightens out for a long stretch, the town commands one of the state's most impressive panoramas. Today Lexington is probably best known for the Civil War's Battle of Lexington, September 18-20, 1861, won by confederate forces commanded by General Sterling Price. The general had moved on the Union-held town after his victory at Wilson's Creek a month before. A Confederate Memorial Park commemorates the event. A few of Lexington's buildings recall that era, their ante-bellum grace still intact after so many years and so much pain.

Sedalia is not on the big river, but it's exactly halfway between two places that are — Kansas City and Jefferson City. That fact has no significance at all, except in a fanciful sense. One might say that Sedalia's "being where it is" qualifies it to comment on the other two cities: one, the epitome of big-town politics; the other, the home of the state government. Sedalia is famous for raising a lot of commentators. In a state where newspapering has been elevated to an art form, Sedalia is the wellspring, the fountainhead of writers for the press of the state and the nation.

Back again to the river. Boonville comes along midway through the state, and is named, without the final "e", for Daniel Boone, who spent his later years in the region. It's another of Missouri's smallish older towns that seem to have stabilized their populations. Built high on river bluffs, Boonville was settled very early in the southeastern limit of the western plains, it gained early importance as a market town for the southern part of Missouri. A pivotal Civil War skirmish, the first land battle of the war, was fought a few miles to the south. This first Federal victory is believed to have kept Missouri in the ranks of Union states.

The town lies in the rich central Missouri river country that has contributed so abundantly to the storehouse of our national history. Boone's Lick is here, upriver on the other side of a bend from Boonville. It's the site of a mineral spring where the famous explorer is supposed to have made salt. Whether he did or not is unimportant. What is provable is that he really did live here during the latter years of his life. Quite a few states claim Daniel Boone as a resident, but two states, Pennsylvania and Missouri, are unquestionably where, in the former case, he was born, and in the latter, where he died.

The towns of Howard County, across the river from Boonville, are all old, laid out in the first half of the 19th century. New Franklin, Fayette, and Glasgow still retain signs of their earlier years and still sit in the midst of the grain fields, orchards, and pasturelands that have cradled them since their beginnings. Like Boonville, they have preserved some ante-bellum homes. Red brick structures, with elaborate ornamentation and displaying great dignity, are relics of the slave-based culture that was imported into the Boone's Lick country from Virginia, Kentucky, and Tennessee. This is still an agricultural heartland, the way it was then . . . rich Missouri River bottom land that yields up staple commodities without much coaxing.

Boone County is a few miles east. Columbia, its county seat, is right in the center of it. Columbia has grown into one of Missouri's bigger towns, fattening on the enrollment at the main campus of the University of Missouri in town. The university's agricultural college has a lot to do with helping the farmers of the Boone's Lick country and elsewhere in Missouri get the most out of their fertile land. Columbia is a pleasant college town, removed a sedate ten miles or so from the banks of the boisterous Missouri River. The town likes to call itself the "Athens of the Midwest" and indeed academia spreads around the community in great profusion. Two other colleges share this address with the state university.

One of the river towns with a difference is the state capital, 30 miles almost due south of Columbia. Jefferson City, "Jeff City" to Missourians, sits high on the south bank of the river. Its great domed capitol building is the centerpiece of a dignified cluster of government buildings. The marble for the Italian Renaissance Capitol was contributed by Carthage, the western Missouri town named for the North African one. Fine stone has been quarried and cut there for a good many years. In Missouri, as in other states, the capital city had to fight for the privilege of becoming (and remaining) the seat of government. Jeff City and Sedalia, 61 miles west, disputed the matter in 1895, but a popular vote the next year scuttled Sedalia's claim.

Across the river from the capital, 21 miles in the north bank, are Fulton and its Westminster College, given immortality during the presidency of Harry Truman as the site of Winston Churchill's remarkable "Iron Curtain" speech, shortly after the end of World War II. Little Fulton not only got Winston Churchill, but, later on, an actual church from Britain. Churchill didn't stay, but the church did, a 12th- century edifice moved from its site in Great Britain and transplanted piece by piece to the campus of Westminster College, in honor of Churchill.

This far east in Missouri, one still feels the pull of the world. The customs and traditions of families who have lived here through many generations, in some case, preserve the flavor of their European backgrounds. Hermann, a river town on the south bank, is an apt example of the old-world cosmopolitanism that was and still is a feature of life in many river settlements of eastern Missouri. Hermann, to nobody's surprise, is a German community, evoking images of the old country from where it sits in a pretty little valley. The town was organized by Philadelphia Germans in 1837 as a way to preserve Germanic traditions and culture in a setting removed from dominant English-oriented society of the East. The Germanic customs endure, in the look of the town, in its festivals, and particularly in its famous Stone Hill Winery and wine cellars. The Winery was the first such establishment in Missouri, producing from the beginning some of the state's finest wines.

Downstream toward St. Louis is Washington, bigger than Hermann, but with the same kind of Germanic personality. Its citizens live along narrow streets that follow hills rising steeply from the river. Their houses are mostly red brick, with the elegance of simplicity, and set level with the sidewalk. Washington was settled by German families a few years before Hermann and quickly became an important river port. That situation, and the arrival of the railroad in the 1850s brought a more cosmopolitan population to the town. Still, the German practices survive, especially in holiday preparations and celebrations.

At this point the big river is getting ready to give up its life to the

Mississippi, thereby turning that stream into a bigger one. But first it has to flow between St. Charles and the outer reaches of St. Louis, both a few miles east. North of the latter city, it does, indeed, come to the end of its long journey.

St. Charles is still town-size, although it once had ambitions to be big-time, like St. Louis across the river from it. A commanding river location and the town's early position as an outpost of the western movement encouraged the feeling that growth had no limits. But by the middle of the last century, the frontier had moved westward and river traffic had succumbed to the railroad's supremacy. So St. Charles, counting some 42,000 people living on its river bluffs, is now a quiet community whose business is still mainly agricultural, but whose historical pedigree and handsome demeanor give it unusual distinction. Like many Mississippi River settlements, it had French or Spanish beginnings, later undergoing a wave of German immigration. Louis Blanchette, a French-Canadian trapper and hunter, is believed to have been first on the scene in 1769, drawn by the high ground of the site, the first such west of the junction of the two rivers. The town received a Spanish name, *San Carlos del Misuri*, after its Roman Catholic church received the blessing of the archbishop of Milan in 1791. St. Charles became the accepted version after 1803.

Among American arrivals, during the period when settlers of many nationalities passed through town, was Daniel Boone with his family and other relatives. The Boones led in the agricultural development of the surrounding Missouri River bottomlands and valleys. Later on St. Charles became the territorial capital and then the state capital. The old capital building, erected in 1814, still stands, three joined brick structures downtown. St. Charles found out in a hurry that legislators, however worthy, do not have an abundance of cash (not in those days, at least). The town's innkeepers reaped no bonanza in the business of the lawmakers, and St. Charles did not go into mourning when the state government was moved to Jefferson City in 1826. All the national strains represented in St. Charles have had some part in shaping the town. The Germans have dominated, by sheer force of numbers. The great stream began in 1829 and continued for about 40 years, fueled by the enthusiastic descriptions of those who had come earlier. The hard-working Germans set the course for St. Charles' future direction, with emphasis on an agriculture-related economy.

St. Louis, and Company

Named for Louis IX, France's Crusader king, St. Louis was founded as a trading post in 1764 by fur trader Pierre Laclede. The remoteness of the setting, in the heart of Indian country, didn't prevent the new village from quickly becoming one of the world's busiest markets. From the outset St. Louis concentrated on commerce, its economic ambitions getting a boost in the early years when Frenchmen, living to the east of the Mississippi, crossed the river to escape British rule.

St. Louis was already the commercial center of the west, by the time of the American Revolution. It assumed strategic importance during that struggle. British attempts to reduce it were repulsed by the inhabitants, Spanish, French, and American colonists cooperating in the successful effort to keep the Mississippi-Ohio river supply route open. For a short time after the war, river pirates preyed on Mississippi commerce. They were effectively dealt with in 1788, and St. Louis began a phenomenal period of growth in wealth and population. French and Spanish culture was reflected in the grandiose homes of wealthy merchants who filled them with furniture, fine china, and art from those European countries.

After the Louisiana Purchase in 1803, St. Louis lost its lonely isolation. It was abruptly engulfed in the tide of Americans pouring into the western territories. The older cultures of St. Louis were submerged under the flood of immigrants of every description, opinion, and morality. For a number of years, a boom-town atmosphere prevailed, with brawling, gambling, and killings frequent along the river levee. But the town began to settle down by the time of its incorporation in 1808. In the next few decades, it grew back from the river, and by 1840 settlers from the East had pushed its population to more than 16,000. As farm lands developed in eastern Missouri, St. Louis became a busy shipper of meats, produce, grains, and fruit to New Orleans.

When the steamboat appeared in force on the Mississippi, St. Louis zoomed in a few years to major-city status. A huge German migration started in 1832 gave the town's young industries a strong push, and soon the city was well embarked on the industrial diversification that has characterized its continuing success. After the Civil War steamboating declined, but St. Louis was more than ever the big knot that tied the transportation system together. By this time it was railroads and river barges that moved the goods.

When the steamboat era ended, the city's river front declined. By the 20th century it had deteriorated into a civic eyesore. But in the second half of the century, St. Louis has created something dynamic and exciting on the river bank where it began. Down by the Mississippi, the Jefferson National Memorial, with its far-reaching Gateway Arch, celebrates the nation's westward drive and the city's role in it. Other parts of the river front and downtown have been renovated and restored, in keeping with the evolving community where culture and history are so important.

Other Missouri towns on the Mississippi have their own special identifying marks. Hannibal, upstream from St. Louis a hundred miles, is a fantasy place as much as a real one. The town, the way it is thought about today, is a creation of Missouri's most celebrated man of letters, Mark Twain. *The Adventures of Tom Sawyer* are the adventures of Twain when he was young Sam Clemens growing up harum-scarum in Hannibal. Clemens was neither born there nor did he remain there as an adult, but Hannibal claims his spirit. It's a legitimate claim, despite some of the commercial, self-conscious reminders to tourists of the Twain connection. Twain memorabilia are everywhere, embodied in a house or building or some other artifact. But more important than these is the feeling that Tom Sawyer could continue his adventures here today, much as formerly. The town has about 18,000 residents currently, and extends far back from the original Hannibal, which grew up along the big river and snapped to attention whenever a steamboat came into view. But the river front is still there, along with the woods and caves and enclosing hills. In summer, especially, Hannibal does not seem so far from the drowsy little place re-created by Twain in his novels and in *Life on the Mississippi*. The beautiful, soft, half-real countryside of Tom Sawyer and Huckleberry Finn is still there. The woods, hills, valleys, and caves of northeast Missouri still spread along the great river. Countless spirited creeks turn around in those hills and pour through those valleys on their way to the Mississippi. They are still full of hidden places where the world is shut out, spooky places where today's Toms and Hucks have their own adventures.

South of St. Louis, Missouri has river towns that are like a taste of Old Gaul nourished in the United States. That, in a way, is what they are, outposts of France in the New World. They started out that way and they still hold onto a great deal of their original character. Two important bastions of Gallic culture and tradition are St. Genevieve and Cape Girardeau, one rather small and the other quite large.

Ste. Genevieve comes along about fifty miles downstream and has some very strong claims to being the oldest Missouri town, the lead mines in the area were being worked in the 1720s with men from France and slaves from San Domingo (now the Dominican Republic). People from Illinois moved over a later and began farming the incredibly rich river bottom lands. The Creole heritage of Ste. Genevieve dates from the times of French and Spanish control before the Louisiana Purchase. East of the Mississippi was the teritory of Protestant England, and Creoles from those parts found a way of life more to their liking on the west bank. Life in Ste. Genevieve under Spanish, then French rule, was benign and relaxed. Once the Americans took control, it was like a new world lto the simple folk of Ste. Genevieve, who were suddenly presented with all the official-dom and paraphernalia of a highly organized society.

Ste. Genevieve started fast, even outpacing St. Louis for a while. But it was left in the wake when St. Louis got its engines going full blast and when the fur trade and the mining moved to the west. Nowadays the town remains stable, if small. Its historical importance has brought it to the attention of more and more visitors. Some of the original late 1700 French Creole buildings are still there, open for inspection. Other traces of Creole ways linger, in the layout of the lots and the gardens, in the *Jours de fête* (Festival days), and in the Creole speech itself, although that has come near to vanishing. French, Spanish, Germans, and Americans all had a part in Ste. Genevieve's colorful past and have made it a treasure-house of history, giving it a new life in the modern world.

Cape Girardeau is southeastern Missouri's biggest town, the center of commerce and education for the state's "Deep South" country. Like St. Louis it began as a river port, dependent on the Mississippi for its economic life. Now it has industries and services based on its importance to the region. Named for a French ensign who, the story goes, settled around 1720 on the "Cape", a point of land to the north, the actual town was organized much later by a trader, Louis Lorimier. Lorimier moved to the high-bank site in his capacity as Spain's agent for Indian affairs in the territory. The Spanish encouragd immigration, so Americans came in from Kentucky, Tennessee, Virginia, and North Carolina; German families came later. This gave a Southern and German overlay to the established French culture. The blend has shaped Cape Girardeau and colors its affairs to this day. The older town core still has some examples of the Greek-Revival homes built by the Southerners who grew wealthy on frontier commerce. There are also some of the plain structures of Germanic tradition, modest houses of one-and-a-half to two stories that, occasionally, yield to the French taste for ornamentation, with some cast-iron balcony railings.

The Cape Girardeau country, and farther downstream into the southeast, has a distinctly "Old South" coloring. During the Civil War in this state of divided loyalties, the strongest support for the Confederacy was found in the southeastern region. Two inland towns that keep their Southern traditions intact are Sikeston and Charleston, located in Missouri's big bulge just before the "boot heel" country. Both towns are centers of a vast agricultural region of cotton fields, grain, and other crops. Sikeston is not particularly old, having been planted in 1860, but with its agricultural future assured by the drainage of the fertile bottom lands, it has grown up without the art of graceful living.